Elizabeth II

Pietro Annigoni
1954–5
Oil on canvas
The Worshipful
Company
of Fishmongers

Elizabeth II
Portraits of Sixty Years

by Malcolm Rogers

National Portrait Gallery   London

Acknowledgements

This book, and the exhibition from which it derives, would not have been possible without the kindness and co-operation of many people. In particular, we are deeply grateful to Her Majesty The Queen, Her Majesty Queen Elizabeth, The Queen Mother, and His Royal Highness the Prince of Wales for most generously lending works from their collections to the exhibition, and for granting permission to reproduce them. The members of their households have been unfailingly helpful and courteous in dealing with the many enquiries and formalities surrounding the loans. I am greatly indebted to Sir William Heseltine, Private Secretary to Her Majesty The Queen, Sir Oliver Millar, Surveyor of The Queen's Pictures, Sir Geoffrey de Bellaigue, Surveyor of The Queen's Works of Art, Captain Sir Alastair Aird, Comptroller to Queen Elizabeth, The Queen Mother, Sir John Riddell, Private Secretary to Their Royal Highnesses the Prince and Princess of Wales, Wing Commander Adam Wise, Private Secretary to Their Royal Highnesses the Duke and Duchess of York, the Hon. Mrs Roberts, Curator of the Print Room, and Miss Frances Dimond, Curator of the Photographic Collection, Windsor Castle, and to Mr Charles Noble. Public and private institutions throughout the British Isles have responded with equal generosity. Above all, the Worshipful Company of Fishmongers, in an act of notable self-sacrifice, agreed to part with one of their greatest treasures, Annigoni's first portrait of Her Majesty, without which the exhibition would have been considerably diminished. Mr Yousuf Karsh with characteristic munificence donated to the National Portrait Gallery on the occasion of the exhibition an important collection of his royal photographs. Miss Eileen Hose, Mr Gilbert Adams FRPS and Mr Tom Hustler have kindly allowed us to reproduce free of charge photographs in their copyright. Lastly, I must thank Dr John Hayes, Director of the National Portrait Gallery, for suggesting to me the subject of the exhibition, Miss Judith Prendergast for compiling the chronology of The Queen's life, and my other colleagues at the Gallery for their support and encouragement.

M.R.

Published in connection with the exhibition held at
the National Portrait Gallery from 14 November 1986
to 22 March 1987

Exhibition organizer   Malcolm Rogers
Exhibition designer   Alan Irvine

© National Portrait Gallery, London 1986

ISBN 0 904017 73 7
ISBN 0 904017 74 5–pbk

Published by the National Portrait Gallery, London WC2H OHE

Designed by Susan Mann
Edited by Gillian Forrester
Printed in England by Jolly & Barber Ltd, Rugby, Warwickshire

Cover   **Pietro Annigoni** *1954–5 Detail*

Dorothy Wilding,
1952

Contents

Chronology	6
Introduction by Malcolm Rogers	8
Plates	14
List of Exhibited Works	109

Elizabeth II: a Chronology

26 April 1923	marriage of her parents, Prince Albert, Duke of York, second son of George V and Queen Mary and Lady Elizabeth Bowes-Lyon, daughter of the Earl and Countess of Strathmore, Westminster Abbey
21 April 1926	born at 17 Bruton Street, the town house of her maternal grandparents
29 May 1926	christened Elizabeth Alexandra Mary in the Chapel, Buckingham Palace
Summer 1927	her parents move to 145 Piccadilly
21 August 1930	birth of her sister Princess Margaret Rose
January 1932	the family move into Royal Lodge, Windsor
20 January 1936	death of George V and accession of Edward VIII
10 December 1936	Edward VIII abdicates, and is created Duke of Windsor. Accession of her father as George VI
12 May 1937	coronation of George VI and Queen Elizabeth
3 September 1939	outbreak of World War II
13 October 1940	makes her first radio broadcast: to the children of Britain and the Commonwealth
March 1945	gazetted Second Subaltern in the Auxiliary Transport Service
8 May 1945	end of the war in Europe
21 April 1947	twenty-first birthday broadcast on tour of South Africa
10 July 1947	announcement of engagement to Lieutenant Philip Mountbatten RN
20 November 1947	marriage in Westminster Abbey. Prince Philip created Duke of Edinburgh
14 November 1948	birth of Prince Charles
15 August 1950	birth of Princess Anne
6 February 1952	death of George VI and her accession as Elizabeth II
24 March 1953	death of Queen Mary
2 June 1953	coronation in Westminster Abbey
November 1953	begins six-month tour of the Commonwealth

25 December 1957	makes her first televised Christmas broadcast
19 February 1960	birth of Prince Andrew, the first child to be born to a reigning monarch for more than a century
10 March 1964	birth of Prince Edward
28 May 1972	death of the Duke of Windsor
1972	Silver Wedding celebrations
14 November 1973	marriage of Princess Anne to Captain Mark Phillips
1977	Silver Jubilee celebrations
15 November 1977	birth of Peter Phillips, her first grandchild
29 July 1981	marriage of Charles, Prince of Wales to Lady Diana Spencer, St Paul's Cathedral
21 June 1982	birth of Prince William to the Prince and Princess of Wales
21 April 1986	sixtieth birthday

Studio Lisa
April 1940

Returning from her daily ride in Windsor Great Park on her grey pony Comet.

Introduction

In sixty years Her Majesty The Queen has sat for her portrait to more artists and on more occasions than any other living person. Among her predecessors only Queen Victoria was more often portrayed, and then over a wider span of years. Of her namesake Elizabeth I there are unquestionably more portraits in existence, but only a few of these are the result of sittings – that crucial confrontation between the artist and his subject – and this shows for the most part in their lamentable quality.

Several of the most distinguished likenesses of The Queen are the result of private royal commissions – from The Queen herself and her parents, King George VI and Queen Elizabeth – and have taken, or will take, their places in the unbroken series of family portraits which is one of the great glories of the British royal collection. At the same time, the demand for portraits of Her Majesty from public and private institutions with which she is connected – regiments, livery companies, universities and so on – has not diminished, and there are still public-spirited benefactors eager to commission portraits for presentation to museums and galleries. In addition, artists like William Roberts (*pp.76–7*), and Ruskin Spear (*pp.102–3*), working on their own behalf, without formal commissions and without sittings, have produced works inspired by The Queen or the monarchy and its role.

Just as she has been painted, and indeed sculpted, from her childhood onwards (*Fig. 1*), The Queen has also been photographed; indeed, in the case of photography, almost from the day she was born. Over the years a succession of images has appeared from the studios of the leading British society photographers, while the great Canadian Yousuf Karsh (Karsh of Ottawa) has photographed Her Majesty on four occasions over a period of more than forty years. The resulting prints are used for a variety of purposes: by The Queen and the Royal Family as official or personal gifts, as royal Christmas cards, in the design of postage stamps, and for release to the press for publication in Britain and around the world.

Fig 1
Sitting to the sculptor
Sigmund de Strobl
Lajos Lederer, *1937*

In general the studio photographs have marked the major events of The Queen's public life: her christening, engagement, wedding, her birthdays and other anniversaries, foreign tours, and, above all, the Coronation. Exceptions to this rule are the photographs which George VI commissioned from Lisa Sheridan (Studio Lisa) shortly before and during World War II, which, with the apparent artlessness of family snaps, show the Royal Family relaxing in the privacy of Royal Lodge and Windsor Castle. For the most part these commemorated no events of public significance, and presented royalty with a charming informality and freshness. They were widely published, and had the effect of bringing the Royal Family closer to the broad mass of the people than ever before, raising national morale in what were especially difficult times.

Fig 2
The Royal Family meeting the Royal Company of Archers, 5 July 1937
Press photograph

In her spontaneous approach Lisa Sheridan was only a part of a larger movement. Although approved prints from royal photographic sittings were released to the press, this was the great age of the press photographer proper, and George VI and Queen Elizabeth, now The Queen Mother, appear to have recognized and encouraged this from the time of their accession in 1936. It is surely no coincidence that, in paying tribute to The Queen Mother on the occasion of her eightieth birthday, the Archbishop of Canterbury, Dr Runcie, commented: 'Royalty puts a human face on the operations of government'. As a result of her parents' enthusiasm the present Queen has been in the lens of the press photographer from her earliest years (*Fig. 2*), and she has led more of her life than any previous monarch in the public eye. As the reticence of the press has gradually diminished, and with the advent of television, she and her family have at times seemed over-exposed. Recently there have been appeals to the press to show greater respect for her private life and that of her family, but all the evidence suggests that The Queen is in general reconciled, indeed committed, to leading a large part of her life in public; to possessing one of the best-known faces in the world, with the limitation of personal freedom which that implies.

The successful press photograph is the lucky chance of an instant, and it is hardly surprising that the overall quality of such photographs is depressingly low. No wonder that the demand for portraits and for studio photographs remains constant. As a result there is, in the words of one Private Secretary to The Queen 'hot competition for the limited time available for sittings'. Such time must necessarily be limited, for, although The Queen regards sitting for her portrait as part of her duties, it is a subsidiary one. Moreover, the act of sitting (whether it is indeed sitting or standing), which entails holding the same pose for long periods, is physically very demanding. The procedure by which a portrait is produced has therefore been reduced to a well-tried formula.

In the first place the organization or individual wishing to commission a portrait will write to The Queen's Private Secretary seeking Her Majesty's agreement to the proposal. When The Queen has signified her approval of the commission and the choice of artist through the Private Secretary, the artist will then get in touch with the Private Secretary to arrange sittings. The number of sittings granted varies according to the needs of the artist. The Italian painter Annigoni received fifteen sittings for his portrait for the Worshipful Company of Fishmongers in 1954–5 (*frontispiece*), but the number is generally smaller: on average six, with an upper limit of twelve. Sittings usually last between one and one and a half hours, though Michael Leonard, the artist of one of the most recent portraits (*pp.104–5*), needed only two sittings, each of half an hour, in which to take the hundred or so photographs on which he based his final painting. Photographers proper may be less lucky. Lord Snowdon records that, as Antony Armstrong-Jones, only twenty minutes were available for his idyllic photograph of the Royal Family in the garden of Buckingham Palace taken in October 1957 (*p.80*). Consequently he was compelled to plan the composition carefully in advance, and to submit a sketch of what he proposed for approval. He intended to show Prince Charles and Princess Anne holding a fishing-rod catching trout, and, with this in mind, he hired a rod and bought fish the day before. Unfortunately, on the morning of the assignment his housekeeper cooked the fish for his breakfast, and he was forced at the last minute to improvise another solution.

Sittings are normally confined to the times of the year when The Queen is in London, though she has occasionally sat at Windsor in April. In London the sittings for paintings and sculpture invariably take place in the Yellow Drawing-Room of Buckingham Palace; as viewed from the Mall, the left-hand corner room on the first floor, where the tall sash windows provide especially good light. For obvious reasons, photographers have used a wider range of locations. The times of the sittings are fixed some weeks or even months ahead. In spring and summer they are in the afternoon, but in autumn and winter, when the light is less good, they are arranged for 11.30 in the morning.

Dress for the sittings is governed by the artist's wishes, bearing in mind the circumstances of the commission. Sometimes it includes a reference to the commissioning body, such as a regimental brooch. Usually The Queen wears the same clothes for all the sittings, and, in addition, these may be displayed on a lay-figure for the artist to copy when The Queen is not present. The clothes never leave the Palace, and nor do decorations or jewellery, though these too are sometimes put on the lay-figure. A portrait, in whatever medium, usually takes less than a year to produce, though the sculptor Oscar Nemon worked on and off for almost five years on his bust of Her Majesty. The finished work is normally submitted to The Queen for inspection, and, as may be imagined, artists are generally anxious to know her reaction. There is, however, no formal requirement for Her Majesty to give her approval.

The technique of sitting, practised over many years, has become for The Queen an art. The earliest sittings of which there is any record were in the summer of 1933, when the then seven-year-old Princess Elizabeth of York sat to the Hungarian society-portraitist Philip de Laszlo. At the first sitting De Laszlo noted in his diary that he found the Princess 'intelligent and full of character'. Unfortunately, at the second she was 'very sleepy and restless', having just attended her grandmother Queen Mary's birthday luncheon party. De Laszlo, working at speed, overcame this slight difficulty triumphantly, and the resulting portrait (*p.23*) is fresh and vivacious. Nine years later, in 1942, the photographer Cecil Beaton encountered a patient and accomplished sitter. He records how 'during one long, cold, war winter' he was summoned to Windsor Castle to photograph the Princess.

The State Rooms were magnificently ornate with yellow or red brocaded walls, huge portraits and marble busts, and everywhere a wealth of gilt; the tremendously tall doors did not seem to keep out the draughts. The cold was so intense that one's breath came out in clouds of white mist. Yet when the young Elizabeth appeared . . . to be photographed in a fairy-story-like setting, she wore only the lightest of summer clothes. The princess was very agreeable and comported herself through a long day's photography with tact, patience, and a certain subdued gaiety.

Dame Laura Knight, in her autobiography *The Magic of a Line*, recalls the sittings in 1948 for her large group painting *Princess Elizabeth opening the New Broadgate, Coventry* (pp.56–7), and notes that 'apart from the respect for Her Royal Highness then gained, I also appreciated the warmth of her personality, lending ease to any outsider such as myself'. Artist and sitter chatted informally about art and music, the Princess revealing that her favourite composer was Bach. The sittings took place 'in a room hung with gold . . . overlooking the Victoria Memorial', perhaps the Yellow Drawing-Room where sittings are held now, and the Princess made one remark which above all stuck in Laura Knight's mind: 'The view from the window there delighted this young Princess. " I love looking at the crowds gathering when I myself am out of sight," I remember her telling me'.

Curiously, it was a similar remark, made in 1954, at the first sitting for his portrait for the Company of Fishmongers, which stimulated and nourished the imagination of Annigoni. While he worked on his preliminary sketches The Queen began to talk to him 'in a manner which was new in my experience, sometimes speaking English and sometimes French. It was a manner which was informal and warm-hearted, and yet it was royal at the same time'. Suddenly, he records, The Queen said: 'When I was a little child, it always delighted me to look out of the window and see the people and the traffic going by'. This simple sentence electrified the artist, and he felt 'a curious sense of excitement, as though the solution to my problem was suddenly very close'. Immediately he suggested that The Queen change her pose, so that she was looking out of the window, and it is on this slight adjustment that the finished composition and the portrait's emotional tone depend.

Sittings for the portrait were held between October and Christmas 1954, and were for the artist 'a very moving experience'. Never before when painting a portrait had he felt that he understood so clearly what to express in the painting: 'I began to sense what it means to be Queen in a land where the Queen is loved by millions . . . I had to try to get into the portrait the feeling of being close to the people, yet very much alone'. By the final sittings he felt that 'it was I who was the pupil and the Queen who was, unconsciously, showing me what my interpretation should be'.

It is hardly surprising that the result of this collaboration, for such it was, is arguably the greatest royal portrait of the century. Its greatness lies, not in Annigoni's technical accomplishment, though this is indeed remarkable, but in the

Fig 3
Pietro Annigoni
1969
The artist's second, and more controversial, portrait of The Queen

Fig 4
Coronation of George VI and Queen Elizabeth: official photograph
Dorothy Wilding,
12 May 1937

evident sympathy between artist and sitter, which allowed the artist to seize on and communicate through his painting what he saw as the central paradox of the monarchy in the twentieth century: 'the feeling of being close to the people, yet very much alone'. Not surprisingly, he returned to this theme in his second, and far more controversial, portrait of The Queen (*Fig. 3, p.84*), commissioned in 1969 by Hugh Leggatt for the National Portrait Gallery. This was grudgingly admitted by one critic at the time to be 'a passable pastiche of a Renaissance state portrait', but the origins of the composition and the portrait's grave mood in fact lie elsewhere: in the traditional artistic representation of the *Madonna della Misericordia*, the sad-faced Madonna of Pity who shelters her suppliants beneath her wide-spreading robes.

Few artists who have painted The Queen have attained, or indeed attempted, Annigoni's elevated emotional and philosophical tone. Nevertheless, the paradox which he perceived in the nature of monarchy – between the symbolic role of monarch and the human being who fulfils that role – is to be found, albeit in diluted form, in much of their work. Most often the paradox resolves itself into tension between the formal and the informal, a tension for which every artist and indeed photographer must find a resolution.

We live in an age when the very formal carries little of the symbolic weight that it once had. Dorothy Wilding's coronation photograph of George VI (*Fig. 4*) taken in 1937 now seems to many as remote and unexpressive as the most stylized of religious icons, and recalls Cecil Beaton's observation that the Royal Family has been photographed so many times in formal attitudes 'that it is almost impossible to break down the results of their training to stand in line'. Sir James Gunn's State Portrait of 1954–6 (*Fig. 5*) is unquestionably an efficient enough delineation of the external attributes and dignities of monarchy, and indeed uses a formula familiar in royal portraits since the time of Van Dyck. However, to modern eyes, accustomed to the vivacity of the newsreel and the press photograph, it is singularly lacking in impact.

Whatever the limitations of the formal approach, the informal – superficially so much more appealing – also has its dangers. Ruskin Spear's *The Headscarf* (*p.102–3*), painted in the late 1970s, may be seen as an apt comment on this. The subject of the painting is instantly recognizable: The Queen in a headscarf, smiling in greeting, no doubt at a polo match, horse trials or highland games, perhaps presenting a trophy. It is an image familiar from a thousand press photographs, and indeed Spear based his painting on one. *The Headscarf* derives its strength from the gently satirical tone with which Spear invests the familiar subject. He mocks, however, not the monarch, but the press photographer who mechanically seeks out that smiling face and apparent informality, as if to prove by constant repetition and cosy conspiracy of Fleet Street, that the monarch is merely the woman-next-door in disguise.

It is no coincidence that the royal smile, so beloved by the press, is conspicuously absent from the portraits and indeed most of the studio photographs of The Queen. Only Michael Leonard among painters has attempted a smile, and this an ambiguous one, between smiling and speaking (p.105–5). He aimed to produce 'a straightforward rather informal picture that would tend to play down the remoteness of Her Majesty's special position . . . to give the viewer the feeling of having a conversation with the Queen – to convey royalty combined with human warmth'. Although Leonard's portrait is perhaps the most informal so far attempted, and though in mood and tonality it is worlds away from Annigoni's portraits, it is still possible to hear in his reference to 'royalty combined with human warmth' an echo of the Italian master's words over twenty years earlier.

While the best paintings and photographs are the result of the collaboration between artist and sitter, press photographs are for the most part snatched unawares. From the element of surprise they derive their interest and impact, and this in all but a very few cases fades with the moment of publication. They offer little to equal the tenderly romantic atmosphere with which Marcus Adams endowed his pre-war royal group photographs, or that gentle strain of melancholy gravity in The Queen's nature which Cecil Beaton discerned (p.58), and which may also be detected in portraits by Rodrigo Moynihan (p.49) and Savely Sorine (p.53) of about the same period. Such photographs are able to stand alongside the finest portraits in other media, for, like them, they are the work of artists with a profound understanding of their craft and insight into human nature. Painter, sculptor and photographer, working with the sitter, all aim to produce images which will endure: this power to endure depends on their ability to say something of permanent interest about the character of the sitter, as Princess and Queen, and about the nature of royalty or the monarchy. It almost goes without saying that the demand for portraits of The Queen would not be so great were it not for the perennial fascination with, and admiration for, her character. Nor would the monarchy exert so potent a spell were it not for the distinction and dignity which she, like her father before her, has brought to it.

Just as he was completing his autobiography in 1926, the veteran society-photographer Richard N. Speaight was visited at his premises on Bond Street by the then Duke of York, later George VI. The purpose of the visit was to ask him to take the first photographs of the infant Princess Elizabeth, born just a few days before (p.14). For Speaight this royal commission, as for any other artist, was a great honour. It was also one which evoked happy memories, for he had photographed both of the Princess's parents themselves as children. Time and the printer did not allow him to give an account in his memoirs of the sitting, which resulted in the very first photographs of the future Queen Elizabeth II, and he ends on a note of regret, but with a wish for the future:

> *So for the present these things must remain unwritten, and I can think of no better way of ending these Memoirs than by wishing long life, health, and happiness to the little Princess Elizabeth.*

It is a wish which has been echoed by artists ever since.

Fig 5
Sir James Gunn,
1954–6

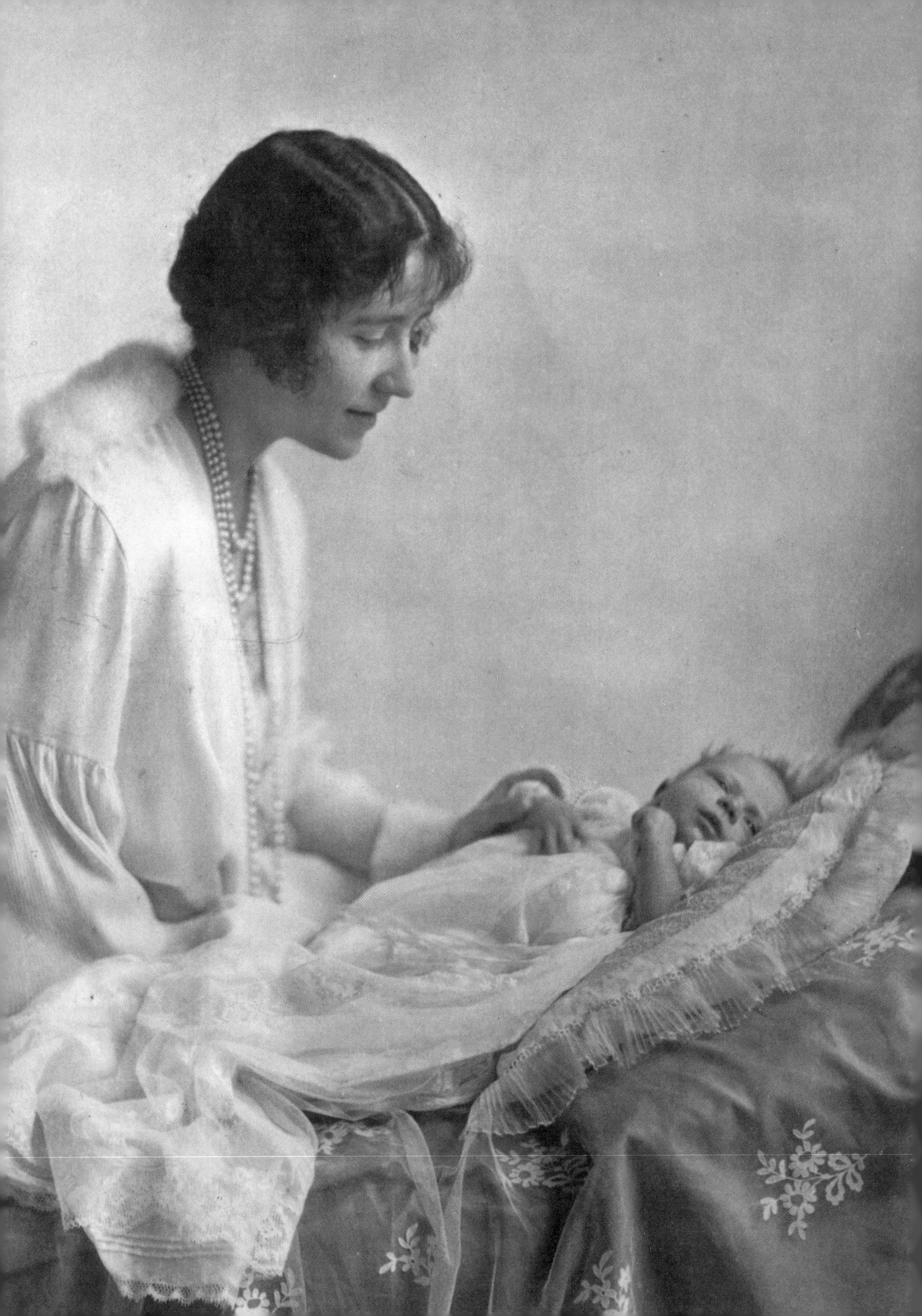

Marcus Adams
December 1926

With her parents, the Duke and Duchess of York, shortly before their departure on a six months' tour of Australasia. The Princess remained in England.

Speaight and Sons
May 1926

Christening photograph, with her mother the Duchess of York (born 1900), later Queen Elizabeth, The Queen Mother. The Princess wears the christening robe of Honiton lace made for the children of Queen Victoria, and traditionally used for royal christenings.

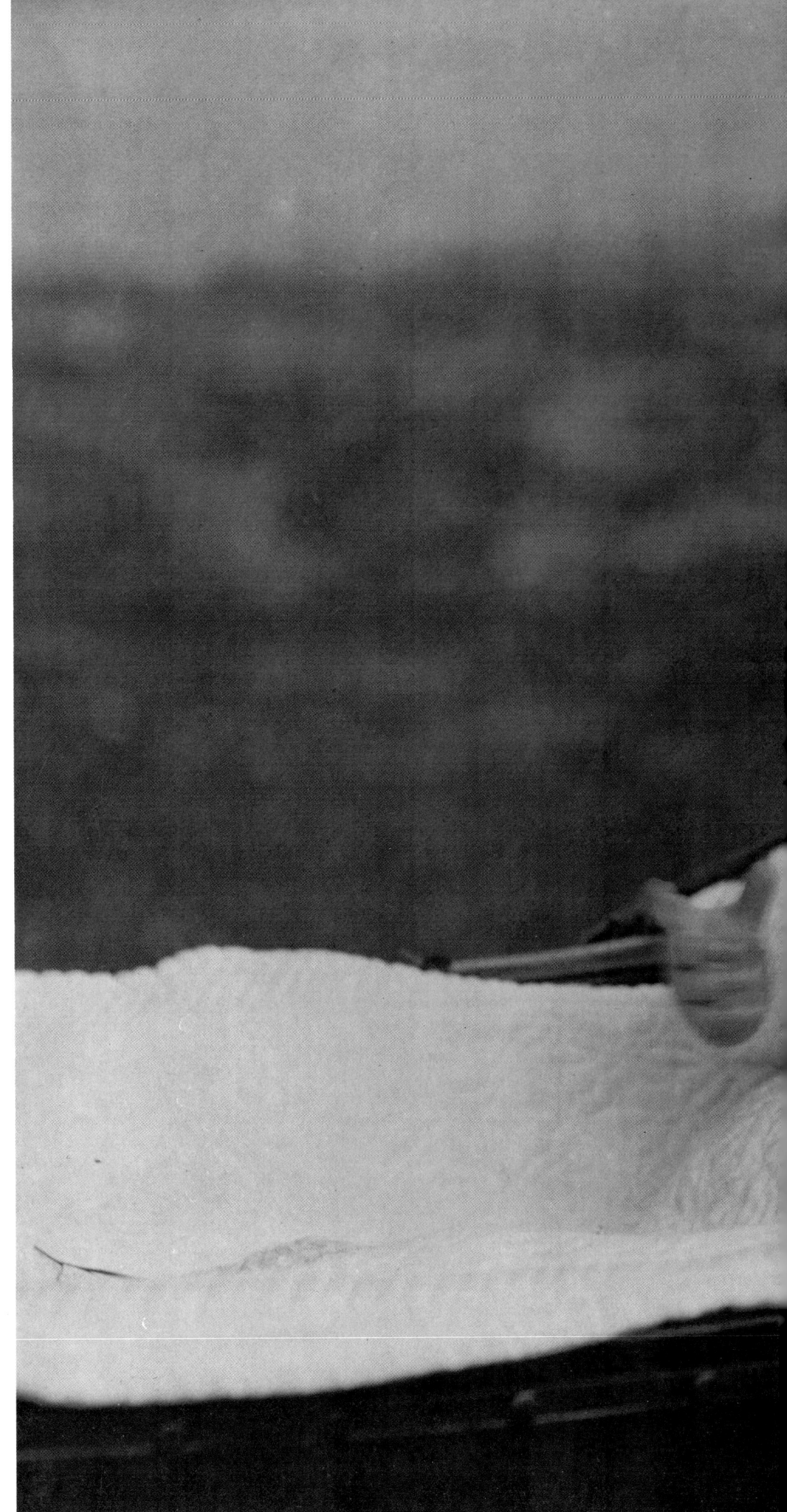

Attributed to
Frederick Thurston
1927

Marcus Adams
July 1928

With the Duchess of York.

Frederick Thurston
August 1932

With Princess Margaret (born 21 August 1930) on a rocking horse at St Paul's Walden Bury, the home of their maternal grandparents the Earl and Countess of Strathmore. The rocking horse had been used by their mother as a child.

The Duke of York
1929

An informal family photograph.

Edmond Brock
1931
Oil on canvas

A characteristically sweet and light-weight child portrait by this little-known society-portraitist who exhibited regularly at the Royal Academy from the turn of the century until 1938.

Philip de Laszlo
May–June 1933
Oil on canvas

The Hungarian-born society-portraitist noted in his diary that he found Princess Elizabeth 'intelligent and full of character', though at her second sitting she was 'very sleepy and restless', having just attended Queen Mary's birthday luncheon party.

Marcus Adams
1936

With the Duchess of York and Princess Margaret.

Studio Lisa
June 1936

With the Duke and Duchess of York and Princess Margaret at Y Bwythyn Bach (the Little House), the miniature Welsh cottage given to Princess Elizabeth on her sixth birthday by the people of Wales and erected in the grounds of Royal Lodge, Windsor, her parents' country house.

Studio Lisa
July 1936

With Dookie in the garden of 145 Piccadilly, her parents' London home. The house was destroyed in World War II.

Sir Cecil Beaton
October 1942

In the Bow Room, Buckingham Palace; Winterhalter's portrait of the Belgian Prince Leopold hangs in the background.

Marcus Adams
1939

The Royal Family at Buckingham Palace. This romantic photograph posed considerable technical problems for Adams. The large group had to be taken with a very wide aperture, which put the background out of focus. He therefore took a second photograph of the background alone, bleached out the background in the original negative, bound the two negatives together, and printed from this double negative. The recalcitrant corgi Dookie was lured into the composition with a biscuit placed on the King's shoe.

Studio Lisa
11 April 1942

Stirrup pump practice by the swimming pool at Royal Lodge, with George VI and Princess Margaret.

Studio Lisa
April 1940

With Princess Margaret in their own garden at Royal Lodge.

Studio Lisa
July 1941

Studio Lisa
21 December 1941

As Prince Florizel in Cinderella, the first of the war-time pantomimes at Windsor Castle, staged in the Waterloo Chamber, in which the young princesses played leading roles. With Princess Elizabeth are Princess Margaret (Cinderella), H. I. Tannar (Baron Blimp), and The Queen. Tannar, a former master at Rugby who ran the Royal School in the Great Park, wrote and produced the pantomime.

Studio Lisa
22 June 1940

Playing piano duets and painting with Princess Margaret in their schoolroom (Queen Alexandra's Sitting-Room) at Windsor Castle.

Studio Lisa
11 April 1942
With George VI in the Saloon at Royal Lodge.

Studio Lisa
11 April 1942
Cycling at Royal Lodge.

Studio Lisa
15 December 1943

Released as an eighteenth birthday photograph. The Princess took the title role in Aladdin, *the Windsor Castle Christmas pantomime of 1943, and wears her costume here.*

Karsh of Ottawa
1943

Released as an eighteenth birthday photograph in April 1944. This birthday was of special significance for the Princess, for it marked the age at which, had she been called to the throne, she would have been considered competent by law to rule in her own person rather than through a regent.

Allan Gwynne-Jones
Princess Elizabeth in
Her Pony Phaeton,
1944–5
Oil on canvas

Presented to Princess Elizabeth by the Royal Windsor Horse Show Club, this painting commemorates the first prize which she won at the Show in 1944 in the non-hackney section of the Private Driving Class.

Dorothy Wilding
1943

In the uniform of a Sea Ranger. The Princess had registered for pre-service training as a Sea Ranger in 1942. This photograph was released on her seventeenth birthday in April 1943.

Sir Cecil Beaton

1942

As Colonel of the Grenadier Guards. The Princess succeeded her godfather the Duke of Connaught as Colonel on her sixteenth birthday. The photographic background is an enlargement of a detail of Fragonard's Gardens of the Villa d'Este *(Wallace Collection).*

Major W.G. Horton
1945

An official War Office photograph. At Aldershot the Princess underwent the NCO's course in the theory and practice of mechanics. She learned to drive all types of vehicle, and practised maintenance and servicing.

Dorothy Wilding
1945

Wearing the uniform of the Auxiliary Territorial Service. The Princess was gazetted as Second Subaltern in the ATS in March 1945: 'No. 230873, Second Subaltern Elizabeth Alexandra Mary Windsor. Age: 18. Eyes: blue. Hair: brown. Height: 5ft 3ins'.

Studio Lisa
8 July 1946

The Royal Family at Royal Lodge.

Dorothy Wilding
1946

Described by the photographer in her autobiography In Pursuit of Perfection *as a '"conversation piece" of the Royal Family in delightful informality around their own fireside'.*

Rodrigo Moynihan
1945
Oil on canvas

Exhibited at the Royal Academy in 1947. The artist was to paint the sitter as Queen exactly forty years after this youthful portrait.

Sir Cecil Beaton
1945
The painted backdrop was inspired by a picture by Rex Whistler.

A. K. Lawrence
c.1958
Chalk on paper

A highly stylized triple portrait which in format follows quite closely Van Dyck's celebrated triple portrait of Charles I at Windsor Castle, though stylistically it owes more to Lawrence's admiration for Italian Renaissance drawings.

Studio Lisa
19 July 1946

In her sitting-room at Buckingham Palace. In her autobiography From Cabbages to Kings *the photographer Lisa Sheridan recalls: 'To get as much of the natural light as possible on her face, I asked the Princess to stand near the window . . . There were constant interruptions . . . while we worked, parcels, packets and letters were slowly mounting up on a table beside the door.'*

Savely Sorine
1948
Watercolour and pencil on paper

A Russian emigré, who had studied in the Russian Imperial Academy, Sorine specialized in very large watercolour portraits, which, with their elegant informality and sophisticated cool colouring, made him popular with English and French society between the wars.

Dorothy Wilding
1947

Engagement photograph, with Lieutenant Philip Mountbatten RN (born 1921), later Prince Philip, Duke of Edinburgh. The couple had been unofficially engaged since 1946, but, on the insistence of the King, the engagement was not formally announced until 10 July 1947.

Bassano
20 November 1947

Wedding group taken in the Throne Room, Buckingham Palace. The sitters are, left to right, back row: Hon. Margaret Elphinstone, Lady Pamela Mountbatten, Lady Mary Cambridge, Princess Alexandra of Kent, the Marquess of Milford Haven (Groomsman), the Bride and Groom, Princess Margaret, Lady Caroline Montagu-Douglas-Scott, Lady Elizabeth Lambart and Miss Diana Bowes-Lyon; front row, Queen Mary, Princess Andrew of Greece (mother of the Groom), Prince William of Gloucester, Prince Michael of Kent, George VI, Queen Elizabeth and the Dowager Marchioness of Milford Haven. Princess Elizabeth wears a white satin dress with train (fifteen feet long) by Norman Hartnell, and the Hanoverian diamond fringe tiara.

Dame Laura Knight
Princess Elizabeth Opening the New Broadgate, Coventry, 22 May 1948, 1948–51
Oil on canvas

Laura Knight writes in her autobiography The Magic of a Line *that this large painting was commissioned by Lord Iliffe, proprietor of* The Coventry Evening Telegraph, *to record the opening of the New Broadgate in Coventry by Princess Elizabeth on 22 May 1948, an event which symbolized the rebirth of the city after the devastating bombing of the war. The ruins of the Cathedral can be seen in the background of the painting.*

Sir Cecil Beaton
14 December 1948

With Prince Charles (born 14 November 1948): christening photograph.

Sir Cecil Beaton
14 December 1948

The photographic background is an enlargement of a detail from The Story of Aristaeus *ascribed to Niccolo dell'Abate (National Gallery). The Princess's basket of flowers brooch was a present from her parents on the birth of Prince Charles.*

Baron
1949

The first official photograph of the Princess to be taken at her married home, Clarence House on the Mall, now the home of Queen Elizabeth, The Queen Mother.

Baron
15 December 1948

Sir James Gunn Conversation Piece at the Royal Lodge, Windsor, *1950 Oil on canvas*

Karsh of Ottawa
1951

Dorothy Wilding

1952

Wearing a sleeveless black dinner dress by Norman Hartnell, and the English Rose diamond necklace, a wedding gift from the Nizam of Hyderabad.

Karsh of Ottawa

1951

Wearing a diamond tiara given to Princess Mary of Teck, later Queen Mary, on her marriage in 1893 by the Girls of Britain and Ireland.

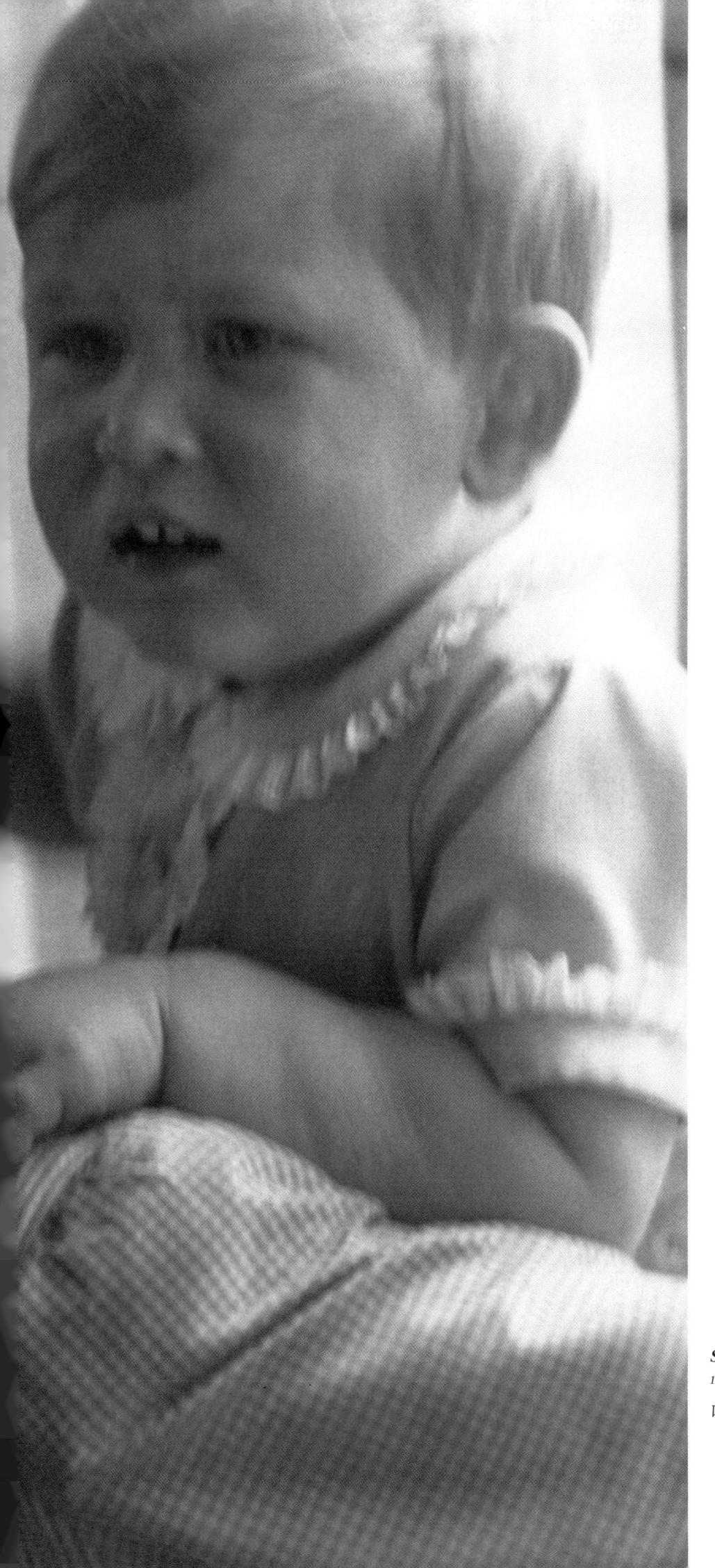

Sir Cecil Beaton
1950

With Prince Charles at Clarence House.

Studio Lisa
28 September 1952

With Prince Charles and Princess Anne at her sitting-room window at Balmoral Castle.

Sir Cecil Beaton
2 June 1953

Taken, like the photograph opposite, at Buckingham Palace after the Coronation ceremony, against a photographic backdrop of the interior of the Chapel of Henry VII in Westminster Abbey.

Sir Cecil Beaton
2 June 1953

Coronation photograph. The Queen wears her Coronation Robes, the Coronation Gown by Norman Hartnell, embroidered with emblems of the United Kingdom and Commonwealth, and the Imperial State Crown. She holds the Orb and Sceptre; on her wrists are the Armills, the Bracelets of Sincerity and Wisdom, and on the third finger of her right hand the Coronation ring. The Garter jewel hangs around her neck. Her diamond collet necklace and earrings were made for Queen Victoria.

Feliks Topolski
Coronation of Elizabeth II: In Westminster Abbey, The Queen Enthroned
1958–60
Oil on canvas

One of a series of large expressionist paintings of the Coronation (together measuring one hundred feet in length), commissioned by Prince Philip from the Polish-born artist.

Sir William Hutchison
1956
Oil on canvas

Commissioned by the Company of Merchants of the City of Edinburgh from the leading Scottish portraitist of the day, this portrait appropriately shows The Queen as Sovereign of the Order of the Thistle.

Sir James Gunn
1954–6
Detail
Oil on canvas

The State Portrait, showing The Queen in her Coronation Robes.

William Roberts Trooping the Colour, *1958–9 Oil on canvas*

Grace Wheatley
The Crown, 1959
Oil on canvas

A pictorial fantasy symbolizing in cheery fashion The Queen's role as head of the Commonwealth of Nations. It was commissioned by the theatrical impresario Emile Littler, along with paintings in similar vein of Prince Philip (The Prince) and Sir Winston Churchill (The Statesman), to hang in the Palace Theatre on Shaftesbury Avenue, where they were familiar to a generation of theatre-goers.

Sir Cecil Beaton
1956

As Sovereign of the Most Noble Order of the Garter. Set appropriately against a photographic backdrop, based on a watercolour, of Windsor Castle, where the annual St George's Day procession and service of the Order are held.

Snowdon
10 October 1957

The Royal Family in the garden of Buckingham Palace.

Studio Lisa
summer 1959
In the grounds of Frogmore, Windsor.

Sir Cecil Beaton
6 May 1960

In the Throne Room, Buckingham Palace, on the day of Princess Margaret's wedding to Antony Armstrong-Jones, later Earl of Snowdon. Wearing a full-length turquoise silk and lace outfit by Norman Hartnell.

Sir Cecil Beaton
March 1960

With the infant Prince Andrew (born 19 February 1960).

Karsh of Ottawa
1966

In the White Drawing Room, Buckingham Palace. The Queen wears the Russian fringe tiara, a gift to Princess (later Queen) Alexandra from the Ladies of Society on her Silver Wedding Anniversary in 1888, and the Garter Sash and Star. Pinned to the Sash are the Royal Family Orders of George V and George VI.

Pietro Annigoni
1969
Detail
Oil and tempera on panel

In all Annigoni received eighteen sittings, and spent ten months working on this, the most controversial portrait of The Queen.
He said of it: 'I did not want to paint her as a film star; I saw her as a monarch, alone in the problems of her responsibility'.

Sir Cecil Beaton
16 October 1968

Wearing an admiral's boat cloak. Taken specially for the exhibition of Beaton's work held at the National Portrait Gallery in 1968–9. He referred to this photograph dismissively as 'the poor man's Annigoni'.

Peter Greenham
Oil on canvas, 1964

An impression rather than a strict portrait, which in its fragile atmosphere and shy characterization recalls the ambivalence of Goya's royal portraits. It relates to a double portrait of The Queen and Prince Philip in evening dress painted for the Welsh Guards in 1962.

Lichfield

spring 1971

At dinner on board Britannia.

Lichfield

spring 1971

Crossing the Equator on Britannia. In traditional manner Lord Lichfield was soaped and ducked by the crew when the yacht crossed the line. 'But', he writes, 'I did have the wit to take a waterproof camera with me and when I came up for about the third time, I took a picture of The Queen up on the bridge laughing at me'.

Lichfield
26 December 1971

The Royal Family at Windsor Castle. The sitters are, left to right, back row: the Earl of Snowdon, the Duchess of Kent holding Lord Nicholas Windsor, the Duke of Kent, Prince Michael of Kent, Prince Philip, the Prince of Wales, Prince Andrew, the Hon. Angus Ogilvy; centre row: Princess Margaret, Countess of Snowdon, Queen Elizabeth, The Queen Mother, The Queen, the Earl of St Andrews, Princess Anne, Marina Ogilvy, Princess Alexandra, the Hon. Mrs Angus Ogilvy, James Ogilvy; front row: Lady Sarah Armstrong-Jones, Viscount Linley, Prince Edward and Lady Helen Windsor. This large group posed considerable technical problems for the photographer. At the suggestion of Lord Snowdon, the Royal Family was grouped round a television (watching a Marx Brothers film), in order to produce a relaxed atmosphere, and the composition was taken as three separate shots. These were later pasted together, and several substitute heads were added at the same time.

Michael Noakes
1972–3
Detail
Oil on canvas

This informal study, finished in October 1973, relates to a group portrait of the Royal Family commissioned by the Corporation of the City of London to commemorate The Queen's Silver Wedding Anniversary, 20 November 1972, when the Royal Family lunched at Guildhall, and when The Queen made her celebrated speech beginning 'I think everyone will concede that today, of all occasions, I should begin my speech with "My husband and I" '.

Ken Howard
1974–5
Oil on canvas

A study for a larger painting The Presentation of New Colours to the Parachute Regiment, *the record of a ceremony which took place at Rushmore Arena, Aldershot, on 15 July 1974.*

David Poole
1975
Oil on canvas

When commissioning this portrait the Officers of the Royal Regiment of Artillery asked the artist to portray Her Majesty as Captain-General of the Regiment. They also asked that it should not be too formal, but that she should wear evening dress and a Royal Artillery cloak, as if she had just arrived to dine with the Officers of her Regiment.

Snowdon
1978

With her first grandson Peter Phillips (born 15 November 1977), son of Princess Anne and Captain Mark Phillips. Photograph released for The Queen's birthday in April 1978.

Susan Crawford
1977
Oil on canvas

Riding on Worcran in the Great Park at Windsor. Commissioned by the Household Brigade, and presented to Her Majesty on her Silver Jubilee. The artist had a sitting at Windsor, when The Queen rode around her on Worcran, and a further sitting with The Queen alone at Buckingham Palace. The chestnut gelding Worcran was foaled in 1958 by Worden II out of Craneuse. He was a hurdler, and had previously belonged to Her Majesty Queen Elizabeth, The Queen Mother.

Norman Hepple
1978
Oil on canvas

Commissioned by the States of Jersey, this portrait shows The Queen as Sovereign of the Order of the Garter.

Ruskin Spear
The Headscarf, *c.1978*
Oil on canvas

This light-hearted study (at one time entitled Blue Skies) is, like much of the artist's work, based loosely on a photograph. It is a gently humorous meditation on a down-to-earth image of The Queen familiar to all from a multitude of press photographs.

Lichfield
29 July 1981

With the Princess of Wales and her bridesmaids int the Picture Gallery, Buckingham Palace, after the wedding of the Prince and Princess of Wales. The bridesmaids are, left to right, Lady Sarah Armstrong-Jones, Sarah-Jane Gaselle, Catherine Cameron and Clementine Hambro.

Michael Leonard
1985–6
Acrylic on canvas

Commissioned by Reader's Digest *in honour of The Queen's sixtieth birthday, and presented to the National Portrait Gallery. There were two twenty-five-minute sittings with The Queen and her corgi bitch Spark, at which the artist took more than a hundred photographs. He based his finished composition on six of these.*

Karsh of Ottawa
1984

With Prince Philip. The Queen wears the brooch made from the third and fourth parts of the Cullinan diamond, known affectionately as 'Granny's Chips', in reference to Queen Mary who habitually wore it.

Prince Andrew, Duke of York
1986

At Buckingham Palace. Released for The Queen's sixtieth birthday.

Rodrigo Moynihan
1985
Oil on canvas

Commissioned by The Queen for her private collection. The artist is best known for his portrait of the Prime Minister, Mrs Margaret Thatcher, in the National Portrait Gallery.

Photographic Acknowledgements

The following photographs are reproduced by
gracious permission of Her Majesty The Queen: 8, 20–2, 38–9, 50, 72–3, 75, 98–9, 106
Her Majesty Queen Elizabeth, The Queen Mother: 23, 49, 52
His Royal Highness, The Prince of Wales: 92–3
Gilbert Adams Esq. FRPS: 24–5, 28
BBC Hulton Picture Library: 26–7, 30–6, 44–5, 51, 68–9, 81
The Belgrave Gallery: 94–5
Camera Press: Cover, Frontispiece, 37, 54–5, 60–1, 63–4, 85, 87–91, 100–1, 105, 107
The Company of Merchants of the City of Edinburgh: 74
Fox Photos Ltd: 9
The Herbert Art Gallery: 56–7
Miss Eileen Hose: 29, 40, 48, 58–9, 66–7, 70–1, 78, 82–3
Tom Hustler: 5, 12, 41, 43, 46–7, 53, 65
The Imperial War Museum: 42
The Officers of the Royal Regiment of Artillery: 96–7
The Palace Theatre, Shaftesbury Avenue: 78–9
Private Collections: 86, 102–3
Snowdon: 80, 97
The States of Jersey: 102
The Trustees of the Tate Gallery: 76–7
Illustrations are from the collections of the National Portrait Gallery, unless otherwise stated

Contents of the Exhibition

Paintings, drawings and prints

Oil on canvas unless otherwise stated
Bold numbers in brackets refer to the pages on which the works are reproduced

1   **Edmond Brock**, 1931   Lent by gracious permission of Her Majesty The Queen (**22**)

2   **Philip de Laszlo**, May–June 1933   Lent by Her Majesty Queen Elizabeth, The Queen Mother (**23**)

3   **Allan Gwynne-Jones**, *Princess Elizabeth in Her Pony Phaeton*, 1944–5   Lent by gracious permission of Her Majesty The Queen (**38–9**)

4   **Rodrigo Moynihan**, 1945   Lent by Her Majesty Queen Elizabeth, The Queen Mother (**49**)

5   **Savely Sorine**, 1948, watercolour and pencil on paper   Lent by Her Majesty Queen Elizabeth, The Queen Mother (**52**)

6   **Dame Laura Knight**, *Princess Elizabeth Opening The New Broadgate, Coventry, 22 May 1948*, 1948–51   Lent by the Herbert Art Gallery, Coventry (**56–7**)

7   **Sir James Gunn**, *Conversation Piece at the Royal Lodge, Windsor*, 1950   The Trustees of the National Portrait Gallery (**62**)

8   **Sir James Gunn**, 1954–6   Lent by gracious permission of Her Majesty The Queen (**75**)

9   **Pietro Annigoni**, 1954–5   Lent by the Worshipful Company of Fishmongers (**Cover and Frontispiece**)

10   **Sir William Hutchison**, 1956   Lent by the Company of Merchants of the City of Edinburgh (**74**)

11   **A. K. Lawrence**, *c.*1958, chalk on paper   Lent by gracious permission of Her Majesty The Queen (**50**)

12   **Feliks Topolski**, *Coronation of Elizabeth II: In Westminster Abbey, Prince Philip's Procession*, 1958–60   Lent by gracious permission of Her Majesty The Queen

13   **Feliks Topolski**, *Coronation of Elizabeth II: In Westminster Abbey, The Queen Enthroned*, 1958–60   Lent by gracious permission of Her Majesty The Queen (**72–3**)

14   **William Roberts**, *Trooping the Colour*, 1958–9   Lent by the Trustees of the Tate Gallery (**76–7**)

15   **Grace Wheatley**, *The Crown*, 1959   Lent by the Palace Theatre, Shaftesbury Avenue (**78–9**)

16   **Peter Greenham**, 1964   Lent from a private collection (**86**)

17   **Pietro Annigoni**, 1969, oil and tempera on panel   The Trustees of the National Portrait Gallery (**11, 84**)

18	**Michael Noakes**, 1972–3	Lent by His Royal Highness the Prince of Wales (**92–3**)
19	**Ken Howard**, 1974–5	Lent by the Belgrave Gallery (**94–5**)
20	**David Poole**, 1975	Lent by the Officers of the Royal Regiment of Artillery (**96–7**)
21	**Susan Crawford**, 1977	Lent by gracious permission of Her Majesty The Queen (**98–9**)
22	**Norman Hepple**, 1978	Lent by the States of Jersey (**102**)
23	**Ruskin Spear**, *The Headscarf, c.*1978	Lent from a private collection (**102–3**)
24	**Rodrigo Moynihan**, 1985	Lent by gracious permission of Her Majesty The Queen (**106**)
25	**Andy Warhol**, 1985, screenprints on paper	The Trustees of the National Portrait Gallery
26	**Michael Leonard**, 1985–6	The Trustees of the National Portrait Gallery (**104**)

Sculpture

Bronze unless otherwise stated

S1	**Sigismund de Strobl**, 1937	Lent by gracious permission of Her Majesty The Queen
S2	**Mary Gillick**, *Model for the United Kingdom Coinage*, 1953, plaster	Lent by courtesy of the Deputy Master of the Royal Mint
S3	**Cecil Thomas**, *Model for the Coronation Medal of Elizabeth II*, 1953, plaster	Lent by courtesy of the Deputy Master of the Royal Mint
S4	**Gilbert Ledward**, *Models for the Great Seal and Counterseal*, plaster, 1953	Lent by courtesy of the Deputy Master of the Royal Mint
S5	**Oscar Nemon**, 1957–62	Lent by the Governing Body, Christ Church
S6	**Doris Lindner**, 1960s	Lent by gracious permission of Her Majesty The Queen
S7	**Franta Belsky**, 1981	The Trustees of the National Portrait Gallery

Photographs

From the collection of the National Portrait Gallery unless otherwise stated

P1	**Speaight and Sons**, May 1926 (**14**)
P2	**Vandyk**, May 1926
P3	**Marcus Adams**, December 1926 (**15**)
P4	Attributed to **Frederick Thurston**, 1927 (**16–17**)

P5	**Marcus Adams**, July 1928 (**18**)		P39	**Bassano**, 20 November 1947 Lent by Bassano Studios (**54–5**)
P6	**The Duke of York**, 1929 Lent by gracious permission of Her Majesty The Queen (**20–1**)		P40–41	**Sir Cecil Beaton**, 14 December 1948 (**58–9**)
P7	**Frederick Thurston**, August 1932 (**19**)		P42	**Baron**, 15 December 1948 (**61**)
P8	**Marcus Adams**, 1936 Lent by Gilbert Adams Esq. FRPS (**24–5**)		P43	**Baron**, 1949 (**60**)
			P44	**Marcus Adams**, 1949
P9	**Studio Lisa**, June 1936 (**26**)		P45	**Baron**, 21 October 1950
P10–11	**Studio Lisa**, July 1936 (**26–7**)		P46	**Sir Cecil Beaton**, 1950 (**66–7**)
P12	**Dorothy Wilding**, 12 May 1937 (**12**)		P47–8	**Karsh of Ottawa**, 1951 (**64**), (**63**)
P13	**Marcus Adams**, 1939 (**28**)		P49–50	**Dorothy Wilding**, 1952 (**5, 65**)
P14–16	**Studio Lisa**, April 1940 (**30**)		P51–4	**Studio Lisa**, 28 September 1952 (**68–9**)
P17–18	**Studio Lisa**, 22 June 1940 (**32–3**)		P55–6	**Sir Cecil Beaton**, 2 June 1953 (**70–1**)
P19	**Studio Lisa**, July 1941 (**30–1**)		P57	**Baron**, 1953
P20	**Studio Lisa**, 21 December 1941 (**32**)		P58	**Sir Cecil Beaton**, 1956 (**78**)
P21–3	**Studio Lisa**, 11 April 1942 (**34**), (**30**), (**35**)		P59	**Snowdon**, 10 October 1957 (**80**)
P24	**Studio Lisa**, 30 June 1942		P60	**Studio Lisa**, summer 1959 (**81**)
P25	**Sir Cecil Beaton**, October 1942 (**29**)		P61	**Sir Cecil Beaton**, March 1960 Lent from a private collection (**83**)
P26	**Sir Cecil Beaton**, 1942 (**40**)		P62	**Sir Cecil Beaton**, 6 May 1960 (**82**)
P27	**Dorothy Wilding**, 1943 (**41**)		P63–4	**Karsh of Ottawa**, 1966 (**85**)
P28	**Karsh of Ottawa**, 1943 (**37**)		P65	**Sir Cecil Beaton**, 16 October 1968 (**87**)
P29	**Studio Lisa**, 15 or 16 December 1943		P66–7	**Lichfield**, spring 1971 (**88–9**)
P30	**Studio Lisa**, 15 December 1943 (**36**)		P68	**Lichfield**, summer 1971
P31	**Dorothy Wilding**, 1945 (**43**)		P69	**Lichfield**, 26 December 1971 (**90–1**)
P32–3	**Imperial War Museum**, 10 April 1945 (**42**)		P70	**Snowdon**, 1978 (**97**)
P34	**Sir Cecil Beaton**, 1945 (**48**)		P71	**Norman Parkinson**, 1980
P35	**Studio Lisa**, 8 July 1946 (**44–5**)		P72	**Lichfield**, 29 July 1981 (**100–1**)
P36	**Studio Lisa**, 19 July 1946 (**51**)		P73–4	**Karsh of Ottawa**, 1984 (**105**)
P37	**Dorothy Wilding**, 1946 (**46–7**)		P75	**Prince Andrew, Duke of York**, 1986 (**107**)
P38	**Dorothy Wilding**, 1947 (**53**)			